Your Unique Journey

A Guide For Your Life

By

Gideon Nielsen

Print ISBN: 10 8799567202

Digital ISBN: 13 9788799567201

Lisa,

Thank you so much for our connection! I appreciate your support, and I wish you well during the work you are passionate about — Caring for others. That is beautiful.

"Be yourself; everyone else is already taken."

~Oscar Wilde

Thank you for being a part of my journey. May you be well and safe on yours.

I dedicate this book to you, the reader, and all the hundreds of people who have influenced my life. I know for a fact, that every single person, whether we crossed paths in a small way i.e. a handshake or friendly smile, or if you were a parent, family member, friend or teammate, you have helped shape the person I am today. Thank you.

Every person is a part of someone's journey and that is why this book is dedicated to everyone who has been an influence on my unique journey.

Gideon Nielsen
Journey Navigator
&
Founder of Your Unique Journey

Acknowledgements

I have a lot of people I want to acknowledge in regard to the publishing of this book, including the friends and connections that have influenced my life to a great degree, and especially the people I have in my life on a daily basis.

First of all, I want to say thank you to my editor Jennifer Ciotta, for her integrity and passion for making this material stand out the way it does. She has understood my vision from the get-go, and that has been a great and comforting help.

A humble thank you, for the outstanding graphic design for the cover of this book, goes out to

Nino and Sun. You are so professional in knowing and creating a red line through the logo, book cover and website, and it all has made me feel very safe in having you take the lead in designing it all. I appreciate your gracious help, thank you so much!

I want to thank Venu Alagh, for her final proofread and helping with the final details, in finishing the manuscript for this book.

Thank you to all the people who have looked through my manuscript and given me feedback; you know who you are.

Thank you to Randi Gonzales for the amazing photo and what became the image that is used as the back cover picture. I appreciate all the photos you have taken of me; I use many of them. Thank you so much!

Deep love and gratitude go out to my parents, Karin & Lars Nielsen. Whether it has been a phone call in the middle of the night, a place to stay or help in any other way, you have always been there for me. You have supported me through all of my risky moves and what seems to be a little crazy at times, and for that I owe you everything. I hope I will be able to return a slight percentage of what you have given to me. I love you and I am eternally grateful.

To my two brothers, Benjamin and Jonatan, who are on their journey through life, I am proud to be your big brother. I am grateful for all the sharing and support we can give each other at any time, regardless of where we are on the planet. I appreciate the way you are and the courage you show in how you go about your lives. You inspire me.

I want to thank the following people for their support, friendship and love:

To a very special person, who has been the person closest to me in the past seventeen months, I appreciate you and will always be humble and grateful for the time we have spent together. You are a beautiful person, with the most amazing eyes, gorgeous smile and a tender and loving heart. I will carry you in my heart, always…thank you.

Jim Kelly, the best coach I've ever had, thank you for our friendship. You are a great person and important in not only my life, but in so many others as well. I appreciate all of our conversations and enjoy sharing and following each other's life experience.

Thank you to Vincent Genna for your friendship and for your kindness in writing such a beautiful foreword to this book. I know we will be on a stage together sometime, and I look forward to it!

To my friend and newfound mentor, Alan Sklar, thank you for giving me direction and help when it comes to professional advice and friendly suggestions to improve this work. I look forward to working with you in the future!

Thank you, Jimmi, for all our conversations. They have all helped immensely. From the very beginning of my shift, you have helped me so much on my journey. I appreciate it.

Thank you to my other families I have around the world. Thank you to the Porter family in Perth, Australia; you are a great bunch and I loved the time I spent with all of you. Thank you to the Hendricks family, as well as former teammates, friends and coaches in and around my other hometown in Vermilion, Ohio.

A warm hug goes out to all the fantastic friends I have stayed with over the past two and a half years. Your hospitality has been so kind and comfortable. Thank you for letting me be a part of your home and my journey. There are so many of you, and you all know who you are. I hope I can give back some of what you have given me. Thank you.

Thank you to all the teachers, speakers, authors and coaches I have had a chance to talk or interact with, have become friends with and/or are now a part of my life, whether it is through friendship or what I have learned. My life would not have been the same without being in your presence and the experiences I've had through you or your work.

And last but not least, a big Thank You to <u>YOU</u> for picking up this book and having the courage to follow what is true for you. I salute you!

Foreword

I first met Gideon at a "Celebrate Your Life" conference in Chicago, IL a few years ago. We sat at the same lunch table with several other adults, Gideon, being the youngest. He looked neat, clean, attractive and young, yet with an energy and air of maturity that distinguished him from the others at the table. Within a very short time, he struck a conversation with the others and me about the conference and different lectures. It quickly became apparent why I sensed such a maturity about him. It was more wisdom than maturity alone. He shared he was from Denmark and spoke with eloquence and insight. There was no doubt I was conversing with a young gentleman, but an older soul.

Gideon shared the story of his youth and how he recently traveled around the world to many places, and at such a young age. I knew immediately and intuitively his journey did not instill the wisdom and maturity within him. His wisdom and maturity inspired and motivated him to take his journey. However, all his experiences gave him the confidence to communicate and share himself openly and genuinely with people from any culture. His journey, as well as Gideon himself, was intriguing and enjoyable.

It was very easy to like Gideon because of his pleasant, gentle, compassionate, caring and loving personality and character. Everyone at the table felt an ease and comfort talking with him as if we all knew him forever. He expressed sincere passion about his purpose and "journey" in life, which was very endearing. So many adults today express criticism about the current younger generation and how they don't seem to have a "purpose" or focus for their future. They've received the branding of the "X Generation," as a result. Gideon is a prime example of how false that claim is. Through his journey experience, Gideon is inspired to help bring people back together in unity and cooperation, getting along as we were all meant to.

We have been close friends since that day. I feel compelled to help Gideon with his dream and mission, since it is a beneficial instrument in helping to heal the world today, and Gideon is authentic in his pursuit to help others. I support and praise Gideon's desire and fortitude to positively impact humanity. In my work as a spiritual teacher and intuitive messenger, I find it healing for people to share their stories and the effects and changes their stories had on their lives. Gideon's "Your Unique Journey" is a way for people to do that. In the dealings of the world today and its residents, you are either part of the cure or part of the problem. Gideon and "Your Unique Journey" are without a doubt, parts of the cure.

VINCENT GENNA, MSW

Author, Spiritual Teacher, Lecturer, Intuitive Messenger
www.vincentgenna.com

Table of Contents

My Unique Journey

I am Gideon Nielsen, and I am your Journey Navigator.

First off, I want you to know:

I am in NO way better than you and you are in no way better than me. We are both unique individuals and that makes us equal!

I have three rules, and similar to the above statement, they will relate to everything we will go through, so that is the reason for their importance. If you need to refer back to them throughout reading this book, then please feel free to do so.

My Three Rules

1. Do what works for you in your life. You have to find your own life path and follow it. Following someone else's path will lead to unhappiness.
2. Avoid putting anyone, especially yourself, on a pedestal. It is a living suicide to put anyone higher or lower than where you are. More importantly, if you do it to yourself, you will nail yourself to the floor.

3. Allow yourself to be inspired by what you read, and apply what you desire. Make sure to use the words, tools and resources in this book as a guide. Your Unique Journey is a guide to finding your own answers and what works for you. The whole point of our journey is that we have to walk it alone. Along the way assistance and guidance are always helpful when coping with adversity and obstacles we will inevitably meet.

With all that said, I hope I haven't scared you away and you're still reading. This book is for you, and my desire is to help and guide you on your journey in life. My hope and intention throughout it all is to help you become more aware of the unique individual you are. It's such an obvious statement, isn't it, that we are unique? Yet it's also something that is often neglected. I want to shed light on this concept and help you rise above to naturally embrace who you are from the inside out.

I would like to take this opportunity to introduce myself, so you can receive a better idea of who I am as well as my journey.

My Unique Journey

First and foremost, my journey and physical life began December 5th, 1985 in Copenhagen, Denmark. I have two loving parents and two younger brothers, all with great character and integrity!

As I write this book, I'm going on my twenty-seventh year and closing in on my thirtieth year on this planet. Even though it sounds like a lot to me, I'm probably what you would consider "young;" however, I feel I have much to share and give to the world.

Throughout my childhood, adolescence and up until now, I've always had a natural awareness, although I was not conscious of it in my younger years. But with this awareness, I also possessed a passion for understanding and studying life. It took off when I was around the age of ten when I began to play basketball. It had so much to do with personal development, and it

2

steered me in the direction of where I am now. For example, even though the sport of basketball was played in Denmark, the terminology was in English. Therefore, this encouraged me to broaden my vocabulary. I built a foundation and acquired an interest in learning more English.

I see the love I have and had for the game as the potential for self improvement, because if you have a ball and basketball hoop at your disposal, the entire game is practically at your feet. This created freedom and ignited my passion for constant self improvement, which influenced the other areas of my life.

Everything in competitive sports focuses on constant improvement. In my case, regardless if I was practicing ball handling, shooting and/or team drills, the main objective at all times was to improve. Thus, basketball was the cornerstone of my passion for personal development.

I developed an unconscious passion for always improving myself. Additionally, I had a curious mind. Before I had two digits to my age and onward, I would always ask my father questions of why I had to do this and that, especially when I didn't want to do something. I questioned traditions, society, work and many other things. I asked these questions, because at that age, I didn't understand why I had to do things I didn't feel like doing. I wondered why other people should be in control of what I should or should not do. I saw that it blocked me from what I felt like doing, which was to feel happy and free. I simply asked a lot of "why" questions that didn't make sense to me.

The three main questions I would ask were: Why do I have to go to church? Why do I have to go to school? Why do I have to work?

My dad later told me that I had my own answer, which was: "Church is for adults."

Like so many other kids, I would've much rather had fun in the backyard, playing games and so on than go to school.

Children do not know how our society works. They focus on what is fun and feels good, as opposed to focusing on what they have to do to get to this point. Think about this concept for a moment. Kids are already there, and when we grow up there is a tendency to believe that we have to do certain things to feel happy. It's, of course, an illusion.

These questions may not seem like much, but there's more to them than meets the eye. I remember that, at the age of about thirteen, when I rode my bike to basketball practice I repeated this idea to myself: "The mind is stronger than the muscle." I would also repeat many other similar thoughts and ideas.

Overall, the questions as well as the thoughts and ideas make sense to me when I look back, even though I have no idea where this natural conscious ability, or whatever you may call it, came from.

I have experienced quite a lot in my young life. Adding life experience together with my conscious ability, it rang true when I heard from a good friend that I am an "old soul," which explains the natural direction I have taken. After my first eight grades in school, I began two years at two different boarding schools. In the tenth grade, I attended the most competitive sports school in Denmark.

Attending a boarding school is very common in Denmark. It's a place where you leave home for a year or two and live at the school. It's a great experience, which helps you grow as a young person.

But my first year in the ninth grade was a rough one. The school was bound by traditions and rules; they contradicted so much of my inherent nature. Although this experience was uncomfortable more often than not, unbeknownst to me at the time, it prepared me for the year to come, which I later saw as the most important year of my life.

In the tenth grade, I attended a well-known sports school in Denmark named Oure. The basketball program is so competitive that almost every year the team competes for the national championship. It's a program that takes players and teams to a whole other level...in one season.

During my time at Oure, American coach Jim Kelly led the program. He had lived in Denmark just short of ten years. He was and is a fantastic coach who understood and, to this day, understands his players and the sport of basketball. He combined this knowledge to teach his teams about this beautiful thing called life. He had already established himself as a top coach and had won and competed for the championship several times. He coached one group of players every year, which means that in one season he actually molded a championship team. Incredible.

The experience I had my tenth grade year was exactly the opposite of the previous year. I had the freedom to do what I loved, because there were far less rules than the other boarding school. However, in the basketball program there were far more rules. I had to be there ten to fifteen minutes before practice began. We had practice twelve times a week. We had to attend all other activities, do both academic and basketball homework and much more. The difference was that these rules were all within a universe that I loved.

Throughout the year, I not only developed as a great basketball player and fantastic shooter, I enhanced my character along with it. Everything spoke to me that year! I was so inspired by what Jim Kelly stood for. He wasn't just a tough coach who wanted the best out of you; his lessons about life resonated with me more than anything. It planted seeds that to this day are still growing and being replanted in the many areas of my life.

Integrity, working hard, showing up on time, being honest and excelling, combined with the idea of being the best I could be, are Coach Kelly's lessons that I cherish. He is a dear friend of mine today as well as being one of the most important people in my life. Without a doubt, he is the best coach I've ever had.

The highlights numbered many during my year at Oure. We won the Danish championship, plus another highly competitive tournament in Sweden. We were the first team from Oure to ever win it. I earned the Most Improved Player award in the basketball program, as well as a nomination for the most improved athlete in the entire school—a school that had many national team athletes from a variety of sports.

That year was better than a dream. Coach Kelly rewarded me with the nickname "Shooter," labeling me as the best shooter ever at the school. I broke shooting records, even achieving the best three-point percentage in practice and in all of our games for the season. I also set a record of making ninety-four out of 100 three-point shots.

It was a beautiful year of personal achievements, which shaped my personality, founded my character and developed a constant pursuit in being the best person I can be, every single day.

After I finished the tenth grade, I worked a full-time job for a year. I worked in a large store in Odense, which was a town close by my parents' house. The duration of the job became a fantastic time of personal growth. I was responsible for a significant portion of the hardware department. The manager believed in me 100%, which was way more than I believed in myself at the time. He trusted that I was capable and gave me the freedom to find my own rhythm. I was in charge of filling up and stocking orders, calling vendors to ensure product arrivals and servicing customers at the electronic department. I also sold televisions, stereos and so on. I performed my job as well as those who had professional training. On the weekends my coworkers looked to me for answers. I was only sixteen years old! Even with all this responsibility and many hours of work, it was a fun time in my life.

The money I earned from this job was going to pay for my dream of becoming an exchange student in Ohio, a state in the northern US. As a senior in an American high school, I wanted to try the basketball environment in the country where basketball originated. So, at the age of seventeen, I moved to Ohio for a year. I ended up living in the town of Vermilion, due to a contact.

While I was at Oure, a former American assistant coach, who had been at the school for two years a couple of years prior to my time there, came to visit us for a few days. One evening, when we were all gathered, he talked about how he had helped other former players from past teams live in the US to attend high school and play basketball. Instantly I was hooked on this idea. I stayed in touch with him to figure out the process. He was from around the Ohio/Pennsylvania area, and his roommate from college was the assistant coach at Vermilion High School. That became the established connection, and from there, the coaches and school helped me find a host family, who was kind enough to take me in for a year.

I signed up with an agency to help with the legalities, including acquiring a one-year visa. They had a saying for their clients, who were young people from all over the world. I remember it clearly and it fits right in with what you are going to read about later on in this book. The quote goes: "It is not better or worse, it is different." When you become part of another culture, this is how it is. This truth comes into play in all areas of life.

My year as a student in Ohio was a great experience and a success in many ways. The reception I received and life I had with my host family was like being a son in a new home and a brother to the siblings. The coaches, teammates and many of the other students helped me to quickly feel at home. And when I go back and visit, it still feels like home.

I improved my English skills, which I use on a daily basis. I became the sixth man on the varsity team. We had the best record the school had had in five years. I developed close friendships too. I received the experience of a lifetime. I often look back at that time in my life with intense satisfaction, because I created all of my experiences and I paid for my study abroad and everything else with my own money.

After I left Ohio and returned to Denmark, two years of community college followed in Odense. I took perquisite classes for university. I moved out of my parents' house shortly after my graduation, and then I began to work for a few years. For the next three and a half years, I held a variety of jobs. Initially, I worked in a warehouse. Then I returned to working in the store where I had worked four years prior, when I was sixteen. I worked there until a year after my graduation.

More or less, I decided to be unemployed for about two to three months, until I got a night shift position at another warehouse for about two months at the end of 2007. I had spiraled downward into a depression at that time. I lacked passion for anything. Work was just work, so I started to live in a closed way. I felt sorry for myself. My "dark period" in Denmark began, but as we all know, before the light comes darkness. The beauty of this time was it awoke me to the idea of uniqueness.

Then in the beginning of 2008, I received a sales position. However, it was short-lived, since it was cold calling to sell a business newspaper to companies and self-employed individuals. I quit, but after about two months, I got a much better and fun sales job in March. It was a job where we lent money to customers and sold electronics over the phone. I stayed until the end of 2009. In the meantime, I researched different ways to invest, how to get in on the ground floor of network marketing companies and how to make money in general. That was the direction of where my life was headed. It was an exciting time, where I developed my entrepreneurial mind, but it was also a time with many ups and downs, to say the least. Most importantly, it began to shape my true desire and passion and that became clearer when a real life shift occurred.

My Shift

On March 2nd, 2009 my life and direction changed completely. Two days prior I had attended a seminar with world-renown speaker Bob Proctor, which had so much valuable information. Enough of it resonated with me and caused my life to shift. I went from a state of confusion and uncertainty to a full understanding of where I belonged in regard to environment, passion and purpose.

It put me on a path, where personal development and spirituality were the key components. Months followed with studying, reading, watching, researching and talking about everything within the two aforementioned categories. I got in touch with myself in a way that I had never experienced or even been close to experiencing before. It created so many realizations, and I woke up to things that I was not aware of on a daily basis. It was a glorious and very invigorating time.

I studied, read voraciously, attended seminars and was certified as a life coach in Florida during the same year. I became a certified coach due to the relationship I had established with the couple who had put together the seminar and arranged for

Bob Proctor to lead the day as the speaker. They were certified coaches and consultants with LifeSuccess and the company Bob Proctor had created; therefore, it became a natural process. I approached the big decision to pursue becoming a licensed LifeSuccess Consultant. It was an intense week of seminars, lectures and loads of studying along with meeting amazing people, who were all there for the same reasons. It was a fantastic experience overall.

I was also investing my money in different areas within the network marketing industry. I dabbled in trading stocks. In addition, I became a co-author of the book *Thriving in Changing Times*, which is a book in the series entitled *Wake Up Live The Life You Love*. I see it all now as an investment in learning. It was actually during that period of time that I associated myself with people who wanted more out of life. They loved to study and improve their lives to a greater degree. I spent $28,000 on that learning period. It was a considerable amount of money, in terms of the place I was in my life financially!

Even with all the studying, investing and learning, I gradually came to the realization that something else was still holding me back. To keep growing I had to put my intellectual knowledge to real life practice. I had to cut loose from my old ways and apply the intellectual knowledge I had gained in the past year. So I followed my gut and jumped into the unknown with a complete focus on renewing myself. And so began...

My Two-Year Journey

Much of what I do, and my passion for sharing and giving, is a result of the knowledge I received during my first year after my life shift and during a two-year development phase, whereby I followed my heart. I threw away all my possessions and left my home country of Denmark. This began a personal and transitional journey, which altered my life completely. It opened a way to build a personal foundation, as well as progress toward newfound opportunities.

It all began February 15th, 2010 when I jumped on a plane in Denmark that was headed to Australia. For some time I hadn't felt well. I was in more or less a depressed state without real direction, and on top of that, I had again, as so many times before, lost on an investment, although this time was the largest to date. I lost $20,000 in two days! Even though the combined amount mentioned before of $28,000 is a larger amount, much of that was a real investment in learning and educating myself, but this was a real loss! It felt like a dull knife had been jabbed into my gut and turned continually. Nothing had seemed to work. I felt that I kept losing, but I wasn't a quitter, though I was extremely close to giving up. This event occurred three days before the end of 2009, but I regrouped and told my parents only two days into the New Year that I would leave Denmark, not knowing when or if I would return.

In the weeks and days leading up to my departure, I sold and gave away everything I owned. Only what I could stuff into my backpack came with me.

At this point in my story, you may ask: *Why leave and give away everything?*

Well, my answer is: "You first truly understand something when you have experienced what you know or don't know about it." For example, I knew this experience would eventually lead me to a detachment of material possessions and other discoveries; however, I had yet to experience it on an emotional level. I would not have this understanding until I lived it emotionally and received the experiences.

The past year, leading up to my travels, had shifted me in the direction of my passion for personal development and self awareness. I studied constantly. But knowledge is not enough to understand something; you have to put action behind it to really gain from it. On an intellectual level, I knew this, and this added to why I had to leave and cut loose from what I was used to i.e. culture, family, friends and so on.

Another answer is that I understood that I was able to enjoy and appreciate my life, despite the lack of material things. Plus, I did not feel the need to acquire or desire for any more than I needed. In addition, in my travels I found that giving selflessly and not expecting anything in return brought many wonderful things in return. To be open to what life has to offer while having faith in the unknown is quite an extraordinary experience, because then fear is no longer present.

My two-year journey started in Australia, and eleven months later it continued in Toronto, Canada, Ohio and then in Costa Rica, and most of the second year was spent in the US. In the first year, my purpose was to cut loose from my comfortable and habitual ways. The second year became a pursuit of how I could establish myself in the environment of personal development. That second year, I traveled to many seminars, workshops and conferences, as well as lived and spent time with people who also had a great interest in this area.

My experiences progressed in the development of my project entitled "Your Unique Journey," which allowed me to gather material for my career as Journey Navigator and for this book.

And NOW…

The next five tools will help you to get in touch with and connect to your own uniqueness. The tools will help you to develop awareness about yourself, which you may not have experienced before. If so, that's totally fine.

As you go through this guide, know that you are totally unique and let that be the starting point for you at any time! It's my hope that you'll feel excited about the information, but you'll also become uncomfortable by what you may feel. When you discover certain unknown aspects about yourself, you can rest assured you are on your way. Change will cause discomfort, but becoming more aware of it will make you prepared for that particular part of the journey you have embarked on.

Let's move on to the first tool to ignite and jumpstart your journey in the direction you want to head!

Keep this saying in mind the entire way, which is one of my favorite quotes by an unknown author:

"If you want to go somewhere you have not gone before, you have to do something you have not done before."

May you be well and safe on Your Unique Journey.

Unique Journey Tool

You and Your Journey is Unique!

"A journey of 1000 miles begins with a single step."

~ LAU TZU

We are equally unique.

We are on a unique and interesting journey through life at the same time.

A journey takes us through many ups and downs, peaks and valleys, but all the trials and turmoil will shape the individuals we will become. Our experiences help us grow; therefore, we are a constant work in progress. This is the foundation for a fulfilled and happy life.

I have five chapters to share with you. They discuss the necessary tools to carry with you in your personal backpack of wisdom as you wander. We are all unique, and we can utilize everything we've experienced in life. We can do that by embracing this principle: We all have treasures inside each one of us, which are just waiting to be shared.

A person I admire and wish I had met wrote this before his passing:

"Happiness is only real when shared."
~ CHRISTOPHER MCCANDLESS

In other words, everything or anything only feels real when it is shared.

Defining Journey

What is this journey anyway?

I did a search for the word *journey* on the Internet and found three definitions:

- Traveling from one place to another;
- A distance or course traveled;
- Passage or progress from one state to another.

(Source: http://www.thefreedictionary.com/journey)

These are interesting definitions and they make sense, although it seems these definitions leave out what is in between, which is the entire experience of the journey itself.

You saw this ancient proverb earlier:

"A journey of 1000 miles begins with a single step."

I chose this proverb by Lau Tzu to begin the chapter, because the journey starts or ends somewhere — that is, if we put a label or specific distance on it. However, consider this idea: The distance traveled, or progress from one place to another, never started/starts or stopped/stops.

What if the definition of the word journey is infinite and ongoing?

We are a work in progress, right? So if we are, there's no point in life when we aren't. But how do we know if the work was not already started before our physical experience and continues after it?

I heard Wayne Dyer say this great quote: "We are a parenthesis in eternity." It's fascinating because we think about this physical journey as one that starts and ends. But where were we before, and where are we going after?

14

Spiritual Journey

"We are not human beings having a spiritual experience. We are spiritual beings having a human experience."
~ Pierre Teilhard de Chardin

The word spiritual begins with the word "spirit" and spirit is non-physical; therefore, it is energy. Quantum physics provides evidence that energy, whatever that really is, is what penetrates and permeates everything. Whatever this energy consists of, it must be in everything and have something to do with the creation of all there is.

My point is to simply look at ourselves as beings on an ongoing journey, which we now experience physically. For this reason a journey can be one that never starts or ends. But this physical experience is our opportunity to move closer to something we wouldn't otherwise possess or be able to understand and be aware of. Due to the time, we are the parenthesis in eternity.

On this physical journey that we focus on, I want to make the following statement, which I believe is true and important for all of us to understand:

We have something to share and give, which is inspiring to others, because we are all on a unique journey that no one else but the specific individual is on.

The key to realizing this reality is to understand that uniqueness is a gift to cherish and embrace. Utilizing this gift will be for everyone's benefit to give and share as much as possible with one another.

To achieve such a goal, we have to love, enjoy and accept ourselves for who we are. We must compare who we are now (our present selves) only to whom we were (our past selves) and to whom we strive to be (our future selves). Comparing ourselves to other people should be avoided, as it will dis-empower who we are and how we experience who we are.

The above idea has taken quite some time to wrap my head and heart around; it is and always will be a constant work in progress to understand.

In my own life, I have struggled because I expected that if I reached a certain point, THEN things would be easier, more convenient and comfortable and so on. BUT, of course, it is not so. It's in the present where you can make the difference you want, but it's taken away as soon as you think about a point you have to reach. The moment is constant, and so is our progress growing in it.

To conclude, what I believe to be one of many truths is that this journey we are all on, regardless of where we are going, is a forever ongoing one. We are and always will be a part of an ongoing journey, something that simply keeps going. The miracle is the opportunity to experience it with our conscious ability while we are in our physical form. Our physical life starts in our mother's womb and continues until we pass away. The physical journey is to experience what we otherwise would not. Since we all experience that differently, the unique journey is one to be cherished and shared, as we can only be fulfilled as human beings by doing so.

Uniqueness

To put two and two together, let's look at the definition of *uniqueness*.

In the same way as I found the definitions of the word journey, I also found these three definitions for uniqueness:
- Being the only one of its kind;
- Unusual; extraordinary;
- The quality of being one of a kind.

(Source: http://www.thefreedictionary.com/uniqueness)

Unique Experiences Lead to Unique Lives

Do you remember a time in your life, when a situation seemed to cause life around you to stop and not go anywhere? I am sure that you and I have both experienced this stagnancy because of some negative event. We have felt that everything was standing still, and unable to move at all. Even though it can seem real, it is a fact that life around us is still moving. Though we may not experience this movement at the time, our perception of how we feel inside is what makes us have an experience like it is real outside of us. Of course, we are moving as well, and at some point, we will begin to move and align ourselves with life again. Keep this in mind the next time you experience stagnancy: Nothing is ever standing still and there is always something going on.

In this section I want to help you look at your own unique life, including your pain and challenges. I hope that you will become compassionate and understanding in regard to the immense amount of people who are on a completely different and unique journey. Keep the section headline in mind: "Unique Experiences Lead to Unique Lives."

On your journey so far, what kind of bumps have you experienced?

I want you to think of a few bumps you have experienced in your life. We typically do not like to fail, fall down, not feel good or not progress in our life. Fortunately, we have misinterpreted these messages, despite how real they feel. In moments of great turmoil and confusion, these experiences may appear and feel like setbacks, but they are what help us advance to the next level from where we are, wherever that might be for us. We overcome challenges. The knowledge and insight we receive from doing so helps us to adapt to future circumstances. Thus, we need those experiences on our jour-ney, since they give strength and courage for the next time life throws us a curveball.

The following phrase will make this idea a bit clearer:

"Failure is not falling down, but staying down."
~ MARY PICKFORD

For example, how do you feel about yourself when you look back at your life, especially during the hard times? Ask yourself these questions: Do you feel stronger? Can you laugh at how you behaved? Do you wonder what you were worried about?

Our mind excels at putting thoughts and everything else into boxes. Often the world can look and feel like a fragmented place, with us in it. When we feel lost, we ride the constant rollercoaster of life along with our thoughts. It is a place of mental concepts and identifications with words, accomplishments and attachments in relation to rating and comparison of who we are, situations and so forth. But what we have to understand on our journey is that it's an ongoing experience, of constant transitions in the natural pursuit of evolution and growth. We have to adapt to change at all times and all the time.

View the journey as an experience, where everything, both positive and negative, is included, because if it wasn't, how could you call it a journey? Because it encompasses everything, the journey is all the content we have to fill in as we experience life.

We are always moving. All the ingredients have to be there for it to be a journey, so that we can cherish the journey while we are on it. When we look back at what we have gone through and see the change in ourselves, we can utilize this knowledge to proceed toward the future with more strength and optimism.

But what tools and ideas will help us as we walk the path we have chosen? What knowledge and information will instill confidence and preparation to go through life, in a more conscious and comfortable way?

It's right here, in this book...

Compare Yourself to You

I believe that to receive the most out of the journey you have embarked on, you have to understand that you, as obvious as it might be, are totally and utterly unique. No one can replace you. No one but you is you and being unique is, and always will be, special.

It's easy to fall into the trap of forgetting and neglecting our uniqueness, in terms of the society we live in and how it operates.

It puts emphasis on being the best, looking a certain way or wearing brand new clothing or fashionable shoes. There is also a type of behavior we tend to follow. It centers around what the crowd does, instead of keeping our focus on how we individually desire to live our life. Just because the crowd goes the same way does not mean it's the way you feel like going. We have to figure out where we want to go. When others dictate what we do or we follow them as examples, this causes fear. We can get into the habit of listening to our peers and society and feel pressured into doing what might seem "right" or normal. We can then develop a fear of choosing something we really want that goes against the norm. You have to listen to what you truly desire to pursue in life, regardless of outer influences.

I believe many of us, and maybe all of us to some extent, have a distorted view of our individual uniqueness and have forgotten or are totally unaware that we, as human beings, have a choice inside and out. Because we are not used to this idea of choice, we tend to blame people, situations and circumstances for what is happening to us and how it makes us feel. Therefore, we struggle and keep approaching life from the outside looking in, all the while unaware of our frustrations and their cause. This will all be explained in depth in the second chapter.

Our society focuses on who we are compared to other people and each other. It's so integrated in the way we live, that in the process we unfortunately forget who we are as individuals on some level. Then we neglect the unique being we truly are. Instead, we tend to focus on what we are not i.e. what we do not look like, the amount of income or money we do not have, the status we do not have in our career or society in general, etc. This is often caused because of the unconscious way we look at something outside of ourselves, as opposed to embracing and cherishing the unique individual we are. We have the ability to use our uniqueness to focus on exactly what we want and who we are inside out, which in essence will make us be and feel happy.

In my opinion we should compare our present selves to our past and future selves. The reason is because you can only compare yourself to what is unique and since that person is you, then you must compare yourself to you and understand the reality of who you are and where you are.

Athletes and competitors on a high level often say that the toughest battle is against themselves. They keep cool and calm in the heat of a game or competition, because they are responsible for if the game goes well, not their opponents.

To take this idea one step further, how can sports announcers and commentators rate and measure who is better or worse, when there are only unique individuals who measure up to their own statistics? I believe we can only compare uniqueness to where a person was and is going, and only to that which is measurable because it is the same unique individual. I actually find it quite amusing to hear any two announcers comparing any one player or team to another. They always end up without a real answer. It's impossible to compare unique individuals with one another.

Was Michael Jordan a more successful basketball player than me or any other basketball player? Yes, he was. But is it more important to focus on how much better he is or to embrace his individual uniqueness, how he improved and what he did in the world of basketball?

What about Einstein? Is it more important to rate him against other scientists throughout the ages or simply enjoy and be amazed at the ideas he expressed as the unique individual he was?

Or do you have people in your life who are similar to you in terms of skills, behavior, looks, etc.? The point is we are all unique. If you can be happy about who you are as a unique person, then you will also begin to appreciate the idea of other people's uniqueness and this idea in general. Comparisons and ratings will always take away uniqueness in anything. I believe eliminating comparisons, rating others and anything outside of yourself will help you and the world come together in a more loving and natural way.

We have to let go of this notion of rating anything and focus on the individual, because rating breeds generalization and neglects uniqueness and the reality of who we are. One answer is not true for everyone; it can´t be since we all have unique experiences, unique lives, and therefore, unique personalities and character.

I am amazed at the idea of how we can utilize our uniqueness in terms of where we came from, who we are, what we have gone through and experienced in our life. It's all unique. No one else has experienced what you have with your perspective, and that is so fascinating to me. Everyone is on a unique journey and has a unique experience, and that is truly a gift and a treasure to embrace in all of us. It is a beautifully-wrapped gift waiting to be opened, as if to reveal ourselves to this liberating fact. This is a door into ourselves which is open with compassion and love, as well as a gift to give to everyone we meet and spend time with on our path.

"A life not worth examining is not worth living."
~ SOCRATES

I like this quotation, because I believe that many of the deepest and most invigorating experiences I've had in my life have been when I've examined myself. For example, I faced and recognized something negative that I was holding onto, which blocked a clear passage toward a constructive and positive flow of life. I personally believe that my life is worth living, and that's why I believe it's worth examining.

How about you and your life…is it worth living? This is not to mean that you should end your life if you are experiencing a painful time. But it is to ask yourself the above question to arrive at this answer: Yes, your life is worth living. And you will examine yourself and make the changes that will improve the quality of your life. As you manifest and/or accomplish the desired outcomes, you will feel the sacrifice has been worth it. And you are worth it as well.

Now, you have the first tool in your personal backpack. There are four more tools to come, which will help you on your unique journey.

Before I end this chapter, the section below is important because of everything that will follow, in terms of what you have yet to read, and more importantly, what you have yet to live. You have already gotten so far in your life, and to excel and go further, you must let go of what is not serving you.

The Step of Letting Go

A helpful step is to let go of what does not serve you. We often hold onto negative experiences and they keep us from solid and productive steps onward.

Two factors that I find extremely important are:
- Total acceptance of who you are as a human being.
- Recognition of what is not serving you and letting go of whatever pain you hold onto.

It is vital to examine our past, especially the major challenges, to figure out if these past negative experiences have anything to do with why we are struggling in the given moments in our lives.

What prevents us from unveiling our most hurtful experiences and memories is pain. We are afraid to dig inside of ourselves. We must accept, recognize and face the absolute truths we have seemed to neglect because of the pain they have created and continue to create. When we look at ourselves in the mirror, we face ourselves and move closer to accepting these truths. The goal is to replace what does not serve us with what we want and what serves us.

How?

Letting go is a big deal, because it will release and throw away a lot of what is not serving you. I saw a great quote some time ago that said something along the lines of: "Every day you have to learn something and let go of something."

We all want to improve our lives. If we want to make room for positive experiences and what we desire and want, we have to create space. To do so, figure out what is not helping you in your life and throw it away. Before you can do that, you have to realize what thoughts, emotions and experiences you are holding onto as yours. Understand that if you want something better, you have to let go of any negativity to make room for positivity.

Detachment is a powerful game changer for me. I held onto certain negative experiences; in other words, I attached myself to them. As soon as I detached myself from these experiences, they began to weaken. Soon, from an emotional standpoint, they were gone. You will always be able to remember something from your life, but it is the attachment of the emotion that makes the difference in how it affects you. In other words, the memory will always stay, but the emotion does not have to.

I suggest looking into the understanding of what detachment means. Check out the book *The Way to Love* by Anthony De Mello; it will most likely change your life! Try meditation, yoga, energy work or some type of activity that will help you release and circulate energy. At the same time, you will examine yourself and awaken to life-changing answers. The key is to let go of what is not serving you.

What to Expect From the Other Four Tools

The next three tools will introduce you to three concepts and illustrations that will improve your awareness of yourself. They will create a mental image to bring order to your mind when encountering the majority of life´s challenges.

In chapter two, the second tool is "The Stickman."

In chapter three, the third tool is the "Comfort Zone."

In chapter four, the fourth tool is the "Circle of Influence."

Then in chapter five, with the tool named "Head to Heart," I will focus on the passion, desire and beauty of following our hearts and why it is not a decision to be made, but an instinctual and guided feeling to follow.

I am providing a lot of information at once, so read and understand at your own pace. If you need to think about a tool or concept for a little while, then do so, and return to reading when you're ready. If you want to read the book in one sitting, and then go back and re-read each tool or concept in detail, then do so. Whatever works for you is best.

I am confident that by reading and understanding these tools, you will transcend who you thought you were and perhaps

Exercise #1: Define Your Own Uniqueness

The exercise that follows is a completely free and optional opportunity. I want you to feel free to do it whenever you want and only if you want. I find that if I tell you to do this exercise before you move onto the next chapter, you might feel it is blocking you from continuing to read if you're in a flow. That is why you should do it when you have the inspiration and desire to do so. That way you will receive the most out of the exercise.

The exercise is to help you find answers inside of yourself and be able to express them. It will make you more aware of your findings. Then you can progress by understanding yourself and creating more clarity.

On the lines below or on a piece of paper, write down all of the ways you are unique…and I mean ALL of the ways you possibly can.

Think about the color of your eyes, the appearance of your eyebrows, the tone of your voice and so on. Assess what personal skills, abilities and talents you possess. Initially, this can seem like a childish way of evaluating yourself, but many of the obvious and simple approaches are some of the most powerful. Many times they are new ways of thinking, which will make you aware of yourself in an entirely different way. The last part of the previous sentence is hopefully why you have this book in your hands and why you have made it this far.

Begin writing these things down, and see how much you can come up with. If you feel like it, keep going until you cannot lift your pen or your fingers are too stiff to type any longer. Then you'll be able to evaluate how unique you are as well as your strengths, weaknesses and what you want to clarify for yourself.

The purpose is to get into the mindset of focusing more on who you ARE, what you ARE good at and what a unique human being you REALLY ARE!

Include everything you can. I am sure this exercise will be a great step for you to progress through this book and on your journey in life!

Express Your Own Uniqueness Below

_____

_____

_____

_____

_____

_____

_____

_____

_____

_____

The Stickman Tool

A New Image of Your Mind

"With all confusion comes order."

~Bob Proctor

I have a question for you:

What does the mind look like?

When answering, what image appears on the screen of your mind? Most people, when asked this question, receive an image of the brain, don't see anything or become confused, because no real image appears. What happened to you?

The point is: Our mind thinks in pictures. If I say the words *bird, grass, house, apple, tree, ocean,* you will instantaneously produce an image on the screen of your mind. The images bring order, because they reflect images of what we know and believe to be true. This is the exact point in exposing you to "The Stickman" because it is an image of our mind, one that will bring order. It is an image of you and us, to understand more of who we are, and essentially how we and our mind work.

Look at the picture on the next page and you will find out what I'm talking about.

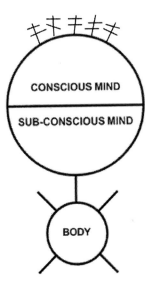

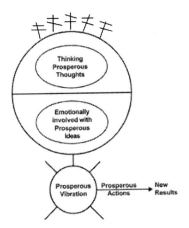

Creator of "The Stickman" ~ Dr. Thurman Fleet (1895-1983), Founder of The Concept Therapy Movement. https://www.concept-therapy.org

Our Conscious Mind

The entire large circle represents the mind. Let's focus on the top half of the big circle, our conscious mind. On the top of the circle and "our mind," you will see what looks like five antennas, which represent our five senses. We can see, hear, smell, taste and touch. We use all of these senses to tune into the world and environment around us and pull information into our conscious mind. Here we relate the information to what our life experience tells us; we compare it and relate it to all that we know.

Our real gift as human beings is our conscious mind. There are three essential keys to understanding and utilizing this part of our mind to the fullest.

The Three Keys

1. Where our free will lives.
2. Where we have the ability to accept anything we want into our lives or reject anything we do not want.
3. Where we have the responsibility for what we think and feel, since no one can make us feel or think a certain way without our own consent.

Our conscious mind is also referred to as our "thinking mind," where our thoughts arise and initiate their effect in the lives we lead. What is interesting, as you already know, is that we think in pictures/images. Understanding this concept will help us to influence ourselves, our lives and what we desire to manifest in them. As we improve our conscious awareness and how we picture ourselves, we will change our lives for the better. Everything indeed begins with a thought and evidently will end up as a result in the physical world around us. After you finish this chapter, you will know that from now on, you will at all times have a say in the matter.

Thoughts	Conscious Mind	Thinking Mind
Feelings	Subconscious Mind	Emotional Mind
Actions	Body	Body

The above table is my attempt to show you three ways of wording the concept. A thought starts in our thinking mind with our consciousness. Then it goes into the emotional mind as a feeling in our subconscious, and through the vibrations from the subconscious, it translates into action, such as behavior and results.

Explanation of The Three Keys

To delve into the three keys, there is great significance in understanding our conscious mind. First we have to understand that the conscious mind is where our free will and the ability to choose are located. Through our consciousness, regardless if we are conscious or unconscious of this fact or not, we have a choice in how we want to respond to everything within our circumstances. This is hard to believe or understand, but with the idea of free will comes the idea of freedom. Even though freedom is relative to any person and what it represents on a grand scale, it does bring about the knowledge that we are free in terms of decisions. We are free in what we say and do, and how we behave from the inside and out.

This leads us to understand that if we have such a choice available to us, regardless of what is happening around us, we have an opportunity to respond in the manner of how we truly desire. We can choose to respond with integrity toward ourselves. We can respond individually in terms of what we believe, rather than with empty and unconscious reactions that often amount to feeling like a victim of our circumstances. Reactions are more habitual and unconscious than responsive behavior, since responsive behavior is more conscious and allows us to be in charge of how we act toward any person or situation. It will bring us a great deal of confidence in how we lead and approach life when developing this awareness.

As we grow to understand the above, it prepares us for when we encounter situations, where people around us tell us certain things or they behave in a way that may make us react. We believe the other person causes our reaction, but the truth of the matter is that this person does not have any control over what makes us react. Instead, we have triggers we are not conscious of; reactive behavior is something we are unaware of. This means that we can establish a foundation of how we utilize our free will. Furthermore, we will become aware that we have a choice in how we behave toward anything. As unique beings, we have a responsibility and a choice in how we act and respond to what happens and enters into our life.

Together with the idea of free will, it is crucial to emphasize that no one but us can take responsibility for how we individually think, feel and behave. No one can, without our own consent, make us act in such ways, because what we have inside of ourselves is ours. We must accept and be aware of when we react and do things we do not desire. We do so because there are things we are not aware of. And because we are not aware, we tend to blame people and circumstances for how we behave and act, until we wake up and face the truths we have neglected to see in ourselves.

The third and most amazing key to understand, especially when we become conscious of this ability, is that we have the gift of deciding what we want to reject and keep out of our lives. If we believe it does not serve us, we can reject it. On the other hand, we can then choose what we want to allow into our lives, because we believe it serves us and can improve our lives. When becoming aware of this idea, we come close to the essential part and the amazing gift of our conscious in terms of how in charge we are of our own lives. If you want a confidence boost and heightened self awareness, this will be a key brick to lay in your personal foundation.

The image of "The Stickman" is a way to have you learn about how incredibly powerful you are the more you utilize your conscious and its abilities.

If we bring in a negative thought or image and become emotionally involved with it, it will eventually end up as a physical result in our lives, which is negative and/or conversely positive. I believe it's where we struggle the most, feel low and imbalanced. It's frustrating because we do not have a clue as to why we act or behave at times.

For example, when people ask us why we just did what we did, we tend to answer: "I don't know." But you know better, right? "Yes," we say. Why is it that when we get to this point, we feel helpless? The answer is probably obvious by now. We are not conscious enough of *why*; therefore, we do not understand our reactive behavior.

To understand this idea better, we have to dig deep inside of ourselves, especially to where we usually do not dare to go. We must wake up to what we've been blind to, and we can only get to this point through becoming more conscious of it. Through repetition we can consciously change what we desire, but we have to understand what it is we want to change and what is not serving us. The only way is to look back in our lives to consciously observe our present habitual behavior. We must replace what we do not want with what we want.

A significant improvement I have made in my own life is the reactionary behavior I used to have toward my parents. I used to defend myself often, because of their comments about some of my moves or choices that either cost a lot of money or were risky. I began to understand and be aware that it was me who was reacting. I had the problem, not them. I began to be aware of it and improve it. If I had listened to what they were saying, I would have answered in a responsive tone with integrity and respect for everyone involved, thus deflating the situation. I would have listened with more of who I am, than who I am not, because just reacting will heat things up even more, which happens without conscious thought. Instead, now I listen and respond, which allows for more conversations overall and more pleasant conversations with my parents. Learning to consciously respond has greatly improved my relationship with my parents and others.

Let's move away from the conscious part of the mind and go into our subconscious. Then we will connect the two parts, which will bring us to what behavior and action we decide and the results we desire. So with that being said, let's move to the power center of operation, our subconscious mind…

Our Subconscious Mind

This part of our mind, as you know, is also called the "emotional mind." It's where we become emotionally involved with what began as thoughts. These feelings are carried out and turned into actions and results through the vehicle, our body.

The following points I want to use as a reference as to what constitutes the subconscious:

-   Paradigm, which is a multitude of habits.
-   The subconscious accepts anything and everything imposed upon it. It does NOT have the ability to reject anything like the conscious mind does. It is crucial to know this, because it will make you even more aware of what you want to allow into your life and what you don´t.

Our subconscious is our database of everything we have seen, felt or experienced in any way and can be recalled in many different ways. It is with our subconscious mind, we can find the information we are unaware of, even though we have experienced it in our lives.

In essence, this part of our mind is where we live out the behavior of who we are the majority of the time. We often hear, that because of the many things that happened to us in our childhood, we have experiences, with both negative and positive connotations, that have stuck with us. Therefore, they have always been a part of who we are. But how in the world did anything and/or everything get to be habitual?

As babies and infants, we did not have a developed conscious mind or life experience, so we basically "without a choice" had our "cup" wide open. I use the term "cup," because look at the drawing of The Stickman again. With your hand cover up the conscious part of it, so it resembles a cup. You can pour anything in the cup, since nothing prevents it from getting in there, nothing can hold it back. There is no conscious knowledge or awareness to relate to anything yet, to decide whether or not any given information from the outside is serving us or not.

The second point is that the subconscious accepts everything that is imposed on it. This means that our subconscious only has the ability of taking what essentially is being allowed into our existence by our conscious mind, since it has no ability to reject anything. Everything that goes into the subconscious is either self-imposed or uncritically taken in by us from an outside source. The Stickman then becomes highly important because it finally gives us the awareness and a departure from the old belief that we are a victim of our environment. We are now able to have a conscious and personal influence over our environment.

Let me ask you some questions: How did you learn to walk? How did you learn your native language? Did you think about the "how to"? Did it happen naturally? First of all, we, as children, did not give up or stop progress, because we didn't even know what failing meant. We kept repeating our action, thus we began to walk and speak. <u>Repetition is key.</u> We learn every single thing through doing it over and over again. To become good at anything, or to learn something new, you have to keep at it, whether it's a skill in a sport, writing, speaking a new language or a change in mood, behavior, income or anything in your life at large.

The word paradigm, which I wrote as a keyword before, is a multitude of habits. What is a habit? Our subconscious is a paradigm, which is all of our habits and where they are stored.

We are unconscious of our habits. We do them without conscious thought. The only way to change a habit is to become more aware of your unconscious behavior by observing your words and actions and then asking, "Why did I say/do that?" And then have the ability and awareness to know why. It can take some time to develop this skill, but it's actually quite fun to be conscious of something you've never been conscious of before because it becomes your own little game. You will begin to feel you're more in control of yourself and you'll choose to improve your life in the direction you desire. This is a positive habit worth developing.

A habit starts by doing or saying something once and repeating it over and over. How did you learn to get dressed or tie your shoes? There are patterns we are not aware of which started somewhere, and that is the reason and cause of habits. When we begin to dissect where a habit or a type of behavior began, we begin a life toward more conscious behavior.

We have to understand that we may have a habit that does not serve us. If we know where it started, that will give us a starting point and a point of reference to replace the habit that does not serve us with one that will. Since we are habitual beings, we have to consciously repeat a new action over and over to substitute what we want in our life, since we always seek more constructive and positive ways of living. It is here we enter the connection between the conscious and subconscious mind.

The Connection Between the Conscious and Subconscious Mind

Since we have the gift of our conscious, and we now know more about it, we will also come to what I believe can be the most difficult concept to understand and accept. I touched on it before, but I believe it takes time to wrap our heads around it, which is:

No one but us is responsible for how or what we think, feel or behave.

We can tend to blame society and/or people and accuse them of being the cause of our problems, of why we feel or react in a certain way. This is simply not true. It is something inside of ourselves that triggers such a reaction. Being aware of what causes us to react in such a way is an open door to a new, brighter and more peaceful future.

At times it's hard to look at ourselves and accept that we really do cause a lot of our own negative experiences, because we are unaware of our habitual behavior and what is fixed in our subconscious. But knowing this will help you raise your awareness to tremendous heights. Keep studying yourself!

We think in pictures, and since we do, we can take the next step, which is to create and visualize images of how we want to live, behave and what things we want to obtain and attract into our lives. The clearer the mental image and the stronger the emotional vibration, the more you can manifest the image you have created in your mind in your physical life. As you perform the physical action, you will see a visible result, and evidently, your new reality.

Imagine your own life and the picture you see. Make it as beautiful as possible! We must begin to utilize this ability and be conscious of this consciousness, which is a precious gift of ours, right?

The more we focus on what we desire as well as how we want to be as people, and the clearer the image we have in our minds, the more we move into that positive vibration. The beauty of this is the conscious insight we gain and the ability to intentionally move in the direction of where we passionately want to go. We have a conscious choice now.

The idea of conscious choice serves as a key to unlocking many of the unconscious mysteries in our lives, when we react toward the world and people around us. Reaction is a by-product of any type of action around us that we take from the outside in. If someone tells you that you're an idiot, in that moment you have a choice. You can believe it's the truth and react, which is a common mistake. Or you can realize and understand that it's something inside you, something that you have not yet recognized, taken responsibility for and understood. It is the cause of your destructive behavior. And you are responsible for this destructive behavior. You are the cause, when something inside is triggered. When you take responsibility for your destructive actions, it is empowering because it stops the blame of outside sources. It emphasizes the choice of what we allow in and what we choose to live without.

Is this tough to understand? I hope it is, because what if people have treated us like a piece of dirt and abused us in all kinds of ways? Isn't it easy to blame those people for the rest of your life? It's easy to continue this cycle, but that pain and suffering remains inside each one of us, and we have to accept it, to move past it. This will also help us in being compassionate toward other people that we meet on our way. We have to focus and implement what we want into our lives, so positivity and constructive behavior has a greater significance on anything that is not productive.

In essence, we forget ourselves when we look outside, blame and compare. We empower ourselves when we look inside, accept what we feel and take responsibility for it.

It is vitally important to understand: NO ONE can make us feel a certain way without our own consent. Live and understand this and your life will change the instant you do.

Change Is Uncomfortable

We will experience a lot of discomfort when changing habitual behavior because we have to get used to something we are not, and that will take some effort. Through our conscious mind, we have to re-program something new into our subconscious and emotional mind. This will make us feel discomfort because it is unfamiliar. When something new confronts something we are used to, it creates discomfort and that is a fact. Every time we step into something new, we do not know where we are yet.

We have to change what is familiar and what is not serving us into something we want. Like learning a new language, change takes time, and initially, during the process it can be confusing. Progress can seem stagnant at times. From changing our income to a significantly higher amount, from depression to happiness, from doubt to faith and worry to trust, changing your life radically takes courage and discomfort. Knowing and eventually realizing this inner power of choice and experiencing it more and more will empower you to change yourself in such a way that you can do anything.

When we begin to grow and have more life experience, we will form a level of conditioning from the way we were brought up to what influences we've had and have along the way.

Even though we have more awareness of choices in what we do and what to do, we seem to carry around the way we were conditioned. When we feel we struggle, even when we are on a conscious level, we know we want to change a great deal. However, it does not take long before that speck of hope is gone because we are consumed with fearful thoughts and feelings. This reality does not serve us, but we hold onto it, mainly because it's what we're used to. Even when we greatly desire change, the pull is stronger than our strength to change our reality. Why?

The short answer is that we hold onto what we are familiar with and that which makes us suffer habitually. We do so because we do not know any better. We are afraid of the unknown. We have fear for what we do not know, but the pursuit has to be reversed, because we must find comfort in not knowing. In the end, we will never know how anything will work out anyway, so we might as well get used to it, thereby creating calmness and peace. This concept will be discussed thoroughly in the next chapter.

The subconscious is powerful and fascinating. There is an infinite amount of information stored in the subconscious part of our mind, along with an endless amount of potential and mystery. We use our consciousness as a way to get to the bottom of things we are not aware of, and by starting somewhere, you can go anywhere new.

The Six Mental Tools

To improve your consciousness even more, we have to cover six amazing ways to improve it. The six mental tools are smaller tools to put inside your backpack as well. I'm sure you know them, but before now, we weren't aware enough to improve upon them. Now that we have an idea of how to improve and change our lives through our consciousness, it's important to implement these six tools. They will raise your confidence even more as you improve and become more aware of yourself as a person and what skills you already possess. These six tools are ways to develop your personal skills, but also to improve and initiate any type of creation you can and want to develop.

When going through all six tools, I urge you to keep in mind what you have read about the conscious and subconscious, because becoming aware of these six mental tools can profoundly raise your self awareness through repetition. Eventually, you will be an action taker who consciously chooses to take positive actions.

Reason Tool

"We become what we think about."
~ BUDDHA

Throughout history this thinking has been a way to explain who we are and the outcomes of our thoughts.

Reason is our ability to think. We know where our thoughts take us. When we reason, we relate, compare and make sense of things we have seen or experienced before. It is a way for us to make sense of anything that comes into our existence. The way reason works is that if you get an idea you can reason with this idea to develop it into something you want to pursue further. You have the ability to choose not to let something in, with whatever type of energy it contains. You can reject it when you believe it is not serving you.

You use reason to figure out what is serving you or what is not. You can decide from that perspective if you want to develop it into something greater or discard whatever it might be, especially if it lacks value. You know what begins as thoughts and continues on through your emotions will result in actions that correlate with what began as thoughts. When improving your reasoning skills, you will become better at gaining clarity on what paths to take, when to reason with certain things and when not to.

You can develop ideas through reasoning. If you get a thought or an idea when using reason, you will create and establish a larger and clearer image of your idea. Eventually, this image has the potential to turn into physical manifestations.

To a relative degree, our reasoning ability intertwines throughout anything and everything related to the next five mental tools and everything you have already read. It's an important factor, something to make sure you pay attention to and focus on improving.

Will Tool

It is in my experience that we all have a fantastic will. When we pursue something of significance we have great passion for, our will is and will always be present when there's something we truly desire to manifest in our lives. In other words, will is consistent concentration, which are the keywords you will put into practice.

Will is the time span you are able to focus on something specific, like a goal or something you are pursuing. It doesn't matter if it's a puzzle, a book or concentrating on a conversation. Our thoughts tend to wander because we are not consciously strong enough to keep our attention for very long in the present moment. Or we have not developed the ability to detach ourselves from every thought that runs through our minds.

Here's an exercise to practice concentrated focus. Light a candle and stare at the flame. In the beginning you may lose focus often and feel you are lacking consistency, but don't worry about that. Simply try again. This is where you practice and consciously know that the more you repeat and do this, you will enhance your ability of concentration. The more your thoughts become one with the flame and the longer you can keep focus on the flame without your thoughts taking you elsewhere, you are improving your focus and concentration. You have the will to stay focused.

You can play around with different ways to practice and come up with other scenarios of how to improve your attention span. Therefore, I will always recommend the following two ways to improve your attention span and awareness: meditation and yoga. The beauty is the two go hand in hand in any yoga practice. Staying centered on your breath in whichever practice you choose will help you become aware of staying present.

Focus is an important skill when becoming great at something or when staying on track with what you're pursuing. We all have a strong will. We have to strengthen it to build confidence in knowing that we can stay on track. Then it will help us to never deter when we meet obstacles and difficulties.

Perception Tool

Perception is also referred to as point of view. We may view perception as how we see ourselves and other people, but also how we view situations, which can easily be altered when we change our view of them or the situation changes it for us. Then we must respond differently.

Our point of view of situations and individuals will always change if we take the perspective of who is in front of us and look into what we do not understand. If we're lacking information to receive understanding, we do know there's a reason why something happened or is the way it is. That's enough to change our view.

Aha! moments come when a light switches on in our mind, and we suddenly understand it. It doesn't matter the size of what it is we do not know or do not understand; the perception of the case has naturally altered along with the Aha! moment. From now on, pay close attention to when you burst out with an "Aha!" because something has made you understand. It's quite fun to become aware of these situations.

Avoid making assumptions or judgments upfront. Figure out a way to see the situation and/or person from another perspective, especially to figure out why s/he is behaving in such a manner. This practice of non-judgment will help you realize that there is reason unbeknownst to you. It will help to keep you from judging and giving negative energy to whatever it is that's happening.

Perception will change our attitude toward so much. When we get sidetracked to a negative place, we can always consciously change the perspective of the particular issue and look at it from a more positive angle. We ALWAYS have that choice!

A way to practice this is to stay alert when negative thoughts and feelings occur. Practice changing your perspective into something positive, as it will naturally alter your attitude about the given issue.

Imagination Tool

"Imagination is more important than knowledge."
~ ALBERT EINSTEIN

I believe Einstein meant: Knowledge is not able to grow outside of what it is. Imagination has taken us to the moon and back. It has developed the evolution of knowledge, by seeing the unseen, which can only be done through imagination.

Creativity and art in any form is created out of the mental images that are unseen to the eye, but we know they start as thoughts and ideas. We are ALL creative people. Many people think they're not creative, but we now know that what you constantly tell yourself will become fixed as habit. Thoughts will hold us back because we have been used to thinking in the same ways. Yet if we consciously choose to focus on the opposite of what is blocking us and realize that we are creative, we start putting action into it. It will become a natural development, as we will begin to substitute something that blocked us from being creative with something we desire.

If you begin to paint or draw a picture every day, write a poem or song, over time you will begin to naturally create and imagine new pictures, songs and things that are only in your mind. All of a sudden, as you mix the two, you will find that your imagination makes sense of the mental images. You will physically manifest the images from your head onto paper, a computer, etc. You will then realize it all began as thoughts. You made the unseen visible because you created a clear image and acted upon it. The more you do this with anything and the more you use your imagination, you have the ability to potentially create anything you desire!

What we really and truly desire is created from a place we can only imagine, which is visible only in our imagination. Here, we can manifest whatever it is into a visible and physical reality. This is already something you have done in your life. Now that you are more aware of it, you can now expand on this further by consciously knowing that it is within you to create any reality from a place that you choose.

My Example: I was at the boarding school Oure, in the tenth grade. Remember when I talked about how I made ninety-four out of 100 three-point shots to set the record? Well, another guy, who attended Oure a couple years before me, had told me he made ninety-two shots. We both played at the same basketball club at the time, and when he told me, I couldn't get his unofficial record out of my head. "Unofficial" because the players talked about; it wasn't in the record books.

I carried the mental image of breaking this record around with me. I played it over and over in my head. During the first part of the year at Oure, I almost broke it a few times, but fell short.

On a Saturday, March 23rd, an early afternoon on a game day, I went down to the gym. I began to shoot three-pointers. Before I knew it, I had made thirty-three in a row. Amazed and confident with the thought that, "this might be special," I continued.

The soundtrack from the movie *Space Jam* was what I had playing while shooting. It helped me get in the zone. I made shot after shot. I got to the point where I had made ninety out of ninety-six shots. I made two more, tying with the record, taking me to ninety-two out of ninety-eight three-pointers made. It was exciting! I shot one more to break the record, and there it was, ninety-three out of ninety-nine three-pointers! I had broken the record! I could have chosen to throw the ball against the backboard, which I actually thought about, caring less about that last shot. But I stayed poised and calm and threw the ball up for shot number 100. It flew through the air and went straight through the hoop. Swoosh! I did it!

That same evening, I wrote the record, my name and nickname "Shooter" on the very socks I wore while making my dream happen. To me it was special indeed!

My imagination had set me on a path to achieve my desired outcome. I have looked back at this moment in my life many times. I know for so long I had imagined breaking this record, even though I was not quite conscious of how clear an image I had created at the time. The clarity in my mind was crystal, so when I had actually made my last shot and was leaving the gym, I was satisfied in a very calm way. Why? Because I had already broken the record in my head so many times. I was like, "Finally! I did it in reality!" This is one example of how powerful the imagination is. It can literally help you manifest the exact image you have in your head in your physical life.

Intuition Tool

Our intuition is often referred to as our "sixth sense." Many theories have been created around this idea, but I want to focus on the fact that we do have intuition.

The word intuition can also be looked at as being "in tune" with a situation. Being in tune with a situation makes you be in the present moment of it and tune in to what is. Make sense?

When we tune into something, we sense on the inside that we are becoming aware of our inner voice. It wants our attention, most likely because something is not serving us, so this inner guidance system of ours helps us to go in a more positive direction, if we listen, of course.

How often do we laugh or comment at someone or something with a negative connotation? Instantaneously we notice a little voice that wants to let us know silently that we should either stop this behavior or apologize. It happens all the time. We hear our inner voice along with the thoughts of resentment, judgmental and reactionary behavior and the way we treat ourselves and our bodies.

We know we have intuition, but do we follow it? Have we developed this skill, to the degree where we really listen to what our body and our soul is telling us?

Without a doubt and more often than not, our intuition seems to know more than we do. When we learn to see intuition as a gift and we trust it, we will have confidence in making decisions and understanding what serves us.

When you sense your intuition is at work, you have a chance to increase your awareness of yourself, what is happening in that given moment and how to proceed. You have to pay attention to your intuition. The more you tune in, the more present you are. Being present will help you deal with situations as they come.

Memory Tool

We all have a great memory, believe it or not…even you! But like a muscle, we have to keep exercising it to make it stronger and better. To make a muscle strong, you have to make a repeated motion in a given exercise, and over time you will create a strong muscle. Remember, your brain is a muscle.

An exercise you can do is to take out a deck of cards and see if you can put five cards down and remember their order. Then go to six and seven. The better you become, the more you will remember until you get all fifty-two cards correct.

You have the ability to strengthen your memory; the more you repeat and practice remembering something, it will become easier. You can even develop your own ways of remembering anything. Imagine your memory muscle expanding as you are conscious of improving it every day.

You should start small and go from there, achieving success by conscious observation and a focus on remembering in a positive mindset. The motivation to witness your own improvement is impeccable. Since you have started small, you will have the foundation to move forward.

To guide you in your progress, I recommend a book entitled *The Memory Book* by Harry Lorayne and Jerry Lucas. It provides insightful ways on how to improve your memory in many different areas, from names to numbers, things and so on.

Exercise #2: Habit Change

The exercise that follows is a completely free and optional opportunity. I want you to feel free to do it whenever you want and only if you want. I find that if I tell you to do this exercise before you move onto the next chapter, you might feel it is blocking you from continuing to read if you're in a flow. That is why you should do it when you have the inspiration and desire to do so. That way you will receive the most out of the exercise.

The exercise is to help you find answers inside of yourself and be able to express them. It will make you more aware of your findings. Then you can progress by understanding yourself and creating more clarity.

The exercise is split into two parts. The first part is for you to come up with the habits you have that do not serve you. To make it easier for you, assign a number to each habit. In the second part, the purpose is to write the habit that is the exact opposite, which will serve you more positively in your life.

Find your own rhythm, but I'd like to suggest what I find useful, which is not initially to write down twenty-five to 100 habits that aren't serving you. This can be counterproductive, since it may overwhelm you with negativity. Instead, I suggest finding your own rhythm, perhaps writing down one to five habits at the most. You may find that taking just one habit you desire to change is the way to go. I encourage you to find whatever works best for you.

You can take this idea further and find something that might not be a bad habit, but something you'd like to change. For example, it can be as simple a habit as biting your nails, or when you sit down with your back hunched instead of sitting straight up, or any major habits like diet or exercise. Choose anything you want to change. In addition, you can try to brush your teeth with the opposite hand, or eat and drink with the opposite hand.

Dress in a different way; watch how you walk or whatever else you choose…

If you are conscious of a new habit that you have desired to change for some time, you CAN! When you explore areas of your life where you truly desire to alter habits that aren't serving you, after completing this exercise, you'll already have the experience of changing habits. And that, my friend, is a confidence booster!

Part 1: Habits That Do Not Serve You

1.

2.

3.

Part 2: Habits That Do Serve You (They are the opposite of the ones that do not serve you, which you wrote in Part 1.)

1.

2.

3.

Comfort Zone Tool

"Life begins at the end of your comfort zone."

~ NEALE DONALD WALSCH

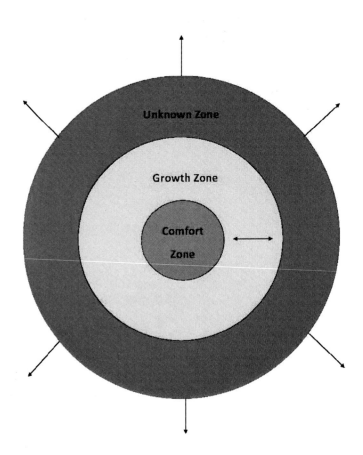

The image I use to visualize the idea, known as the "Comfort Zone," is for making sense out of the obvious. The obvious is where we are the most comfortable. I've made the image of the Comfort Zone, so we can see the inside area as our "actual" comfort zone. It is where we are comfortable and get used to everything over time. It is the ever-expanding part of who we are, such as our accumulation of life experience, knowledge, information of any sort and wisdom. It's everything that's happened to us.

The next zone is the yellow area, or the "Growth Zone." I see this area as vitally important for our life and growth. As we move farther into the chapter, I will discuss the Growth Zone in detail.

Outside the Growth Zone, it is all red, as far as the eye can see. This is the "Unknown Zone." It's where we haven't been, and what we haven't experienced; therefore, we are unable to relate to anything whatsoever. When we feel totally lost and cannot seem to find ground, we can refer to this area and know we're in the Unknown Zone.

The Comfort Zone & Growth Zone

Without further ado, let's dive into this three-part Comfort Zone, starting from the inside and proceeding outward. Let's begin with our green zone, the actual Comfort Zone area.

This quote opened the chapter, but read it again:

"Life begins at the end of your comfort zone."

Through my own experience I believe we thrive, learn and grow so much more when we are at the end of our comfort zone. However, I would personally use the word "edge" of our comfort zone. The more we move toward the edge and expand our comfort zone, the more confident we will grow, since it is a natural process of personal growth. Eventually, excitement will override fear as we continue to explore the edge of our comfort zone.

Abraham Maslow said: "People will either step forward into growth, or back into safety." I believe no one is perfect or done learning and/or growing. We all have a tendency in many different areas and on an infinite scale of levels to stay in the familiar, because we are afraid of stepping out of it and into something that we do not know at all. It is a constant, and something we must face. When trying something new, remember that fear has beauty and is natural.

Our comfort zone can be viewed as our blind side as well, especially when it does not serve us. We resist change because we have been comfortable in our suffering for a given length of time. It seems counter intuitive, doesn't it?

As Michael Jordan brilliantly says: "Fear is an illusion."

When you step into fear, it dissolves immediately!

The goal is to pursue something new, to be able to recognize that too much comfort can lead to suffering, and stepping out of the Comfort Zone is the first step in growing out of it. We hold onto more if we stay in what we are used to and hold onto less when we pursue something new on a more consistent basis. Then we are growing as a person, being and feeling something new within ourselves and also around ourselves.

So how do we get more used to expanding our comfort zone? How do we take steps into the unknown with more excitement, rather than being afraid? These are big questions, and I hope to create more clarity for you around this topic by the end of this chapter.

To do so, I want to merge what we have experienced in the previous chapter, and the concepts of The Stickman and Comfort Zone, the reason being they are connected. What I want to do is connect both ideas and make sense out of them. I want to focus our attention on the discomfort we feel when encountering something new. And we already know it's the subconscious mind which is in play here, right?

We know that through conscious repetition of an action, we will get better or more used to something in a given area. We can then utilize this idea and get into a habit of expanding our comfort zone further by stepping out of it more often.

Over time we'll get comfortable with most people, situations, etc. we encounter. The things that bring us discomfort or we still have to learn we will get comfortable with, but the difference will be, if it serves us or not. Regardless if your comfort is positive and enjoyable or it's a suffering type of comfort, it all has to do with the idea of habitual behavior and how we live our lives. So remember to bring in your conscious gift, to let yourself be aware of it. Understand that we are habitual beings; we have the conscious ability to choose what direction we naturally want to go, either positively or negatively.

Therefore, it is vital and extremely healthy to be in the Growth Zone, where life is happening, with us in it. In my opinion there is no better place to live or be than in this particular zone. The reason is because discomfort is behind all eventual positive and constructive outcomes. The more we can get comfortable with and understand this idea, the better. It will create inner space around how we proceed, allowing for more peace and trust throughout this process of change.

The Growth Zone is where we literally grow, and where both excitement and "down time" meet. Go back to the model and look at the entire yellow section. It's kind of a finite edge, because we are in this area as soon as we step out of our comfort zone. And when we step around the edge of the red, we pull in new and unknown information, which is essential for evolution and personal growth.

I believe we are in this area our entire lives, even though it's relative to each individual how much that is. We constantly grow and we constantly can be in a suffering type of state. We have to understand that the way we deal with things generally is the way it will be dealt with "naturally," or in other words, habitually, as we get comfortable moving into our green comfort zone area.

We are constantly in a process of evolutionary progress of adapting to the new and the change that infinitely will always be with us, and the more aware of this we are, the more we'll let things be as they are. We will take the necessary time to grow and become more comfortable with discomfort and know that it's all for the better. We have lessons to learn at any given time.

The Unknown Zone

As stated above, there is an edge or line between the Growth Zone and the Unknown Zone. It is here where we touch on what we have yet to discover and parts of ourselves we have yet to realize. As we do, we pull in all the "new" we have to deal with to the Growth Zone. Then we will have the potential to elevate ourselves to another personal level.

It can be dangerous and/or frightening to step completely out of the Growth Zone and into the red Unknown Zone because it's too big of a step more often than not. I believe that is why we have to remain at the edge. We must step into the unknown with a toe or half a foot at a time, pull in the new, and then grow and learn to get comfortable with the new. As we become greener (more comfortable), we can step into the red again, and "be on the edge" so to speak. The Growth Zone dictates how long it takes to get comfortable with anything new, according to how big of a new step it is in our lives at the given time.

On our life journey, we cannot avoid that sometimes we either have to or happen to be in the Unknown Zone because of natural circumstances that leave us in immense confusion, stuck and in a struggle. We are left with a question mark as to how to proceed from there. These are the times when we have to draw on all the experience we have. But it's also at the mercy of time to have the patience for us to come together, to adapt and learn from this newness.

This is one of those times in life where we have to deal with our circumstances the best we can when we are in them, and seek advice and support from others if necessary.

Conclusion

To conclude, our green Comfort Zone is where everything eventually ends up, whether it's positive or suffering comfort. The more new we encounter on the edge of the Growth Zone and the Unknown Zone determines the courage we obtain within our personality and the accumulation of life experiences. The more we are in the Growth Zone the more we live and live with purpose.

The more you get comfortable with stepping into the unknown and growth, the better you will understand yourself. You will acquire a natural advantage that will help others during their difficult times too. I'm not sure we can be prepared for the day we stand with both of our feet in the complete and utter unknown. I believe there are times we just have to be in it, the best way we possibly can. We have to take the unique being we are into the unique experience that fits what we, as individuals, have to go through in order to understand or have an important lesson. This will serve us and fit us for the time to come.

In other words, I believe that if we, at a given time, end up with both of our feet in the unknown, we have to rely on the fact that we are there for a reason. It may be out of our comprehension to understand why and what that reason is while we are in the unknown. The reason will most likely not be clear until you have been through the experience emotionally. When you have, and when both the situation and your emotions gradually settle, you will be clearer in understanding the reason or reasons. (Remember that during the turmoil, it's impossible to have this kind of clarity.) By this point we will know we had to go through this turmoil in order to grow and learn something. We will have more wisdom for what the future will bring us.

So now you have an idea of how to begin the process of change. At each stage of your life, you will be able to place yourself according to where you are in one of these three zones and be somewhat aware of your situation.

And if you ever feel stuck, in struggle or hesitation as to what action to take then leave the habitual comfort, so you avoid suffering in it.

Exercise #3: Clarity on Dreams, Fears & Actions

The exercise that follows is a completely free and optional opportunity. I want you to feel free to do it whenever you want and only if you want. I find that if I tell you to do this exercise before you move onto the next chapter, you might feel it is blocking you from continuing to read if you're in a flow. That is why you should do it when you have the inspiration and desire to do so. That way you will receive the most out of the exercise.

The exercise is to help you find answers inside of yourself and be able to express them. It will make you more aware of your findings. Then you can progress by understanding yourself and creating more clarity.

You've heard this quote a few times already: "If you want to go somewhere you have not gone before, you have to do something you have not done before."

This exercise is for you to determine where you want to go, and what you have not yet done to get there. What keeps you from taking action and steps toward the things in life you are passionate about or simply want to do or pursue?

This exercise is to help you gain clarity for your wants and become aware of what is holding you back. You will learn what kind of comfort you are in and what you have to break free from, to step into the unfamiliar to pursue the dreams, desires, passions and experiences that you want to obtain in your life. Something is holding you back and if you can get clear on what that is, you already have the tools to turn this behavior around. That is my hope for you as you do this exercise.

I have split the exercise into three parts. The first part is for you to determine where it is you want to go i.e. goals, dreams and so on.

The second part is for you to determine what holds you back, the type of fear and what prevents you from obtaining your goals.

The third part is for you to determine what action steps or what you have to do that you have not done before to achieve your wants. When you write these down, ignore doubtful thoughts, such as "I can't do this" or "I don't have enough money." Instead write down your action steps regardless of how uncomfortable or impossible it may feel or seem.

This exercise is to know right here and right now in this moment how you see yourself, and what you have to do to progress in the direction of where you want to go.

Part 1: Where do you want to go? What are your goals and dreams? Write down your ultimate desires.

_____

_____

_____

_____

_____

_____

_____

_____

_____

Part 2: What is holding you back? What fears do you have? What prevents you from achieving your desires?

_____

_____

_____

_____

_____

_____

_____

_____

_____

_____

Part 3: What actions do you have to do, that you have not done before, to go where you have not gone before?

_____

_____

_____

_____

_____

_____

_____

_____

Circle of Influence Tool

"God grant me the serenity to accept the things I cannot change; courage to change the things I can; and the wisdom to know the difference."

~ REINHOLD NIEBUHR

When I was first introduced to what I call "the circle of influence" it was named "the circle of control." The word and term control is an illusion, which is why I have changed it to influence, because that is what I believe we are and what we possess, more so than actual control. If there is order in chaos, we must be able to influence who we are and our surroundings inside and out. Many times a lot of what we experience internally can seem like chaos, until we begin to fall into some kind of order.

Before going into the model and information in this chapter, keep the following phrase in mind. I believe it will help you:

"Be the influence you wish to experience."

Throughout this book, you have been given two models so far and this is the third, and I have used these three specifically because they go hand in hand. As you can see on this page, the image looks similar to the comfort zone, but the difference is the outer third circle, which is closed off and excludes colors.

I urge you to pay attention to these two focuses:

- The Influence you have toward yourself and your immediate environment.

- Living with confidence and trust in who you are inside and out.

Let´s get to it!

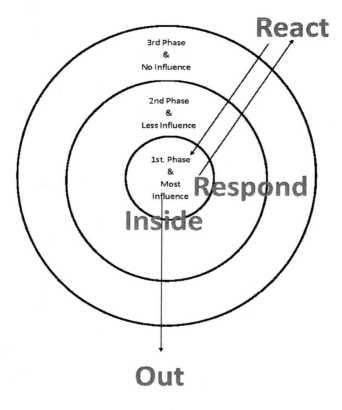

First phase

The inner, second and third circle are the three phases of influence. And again, it is important for me to emphasize to keep the "inside out" mindset at all times. Like an eagle that hovers above its prey, the essentials for how this eagle can survive are determined by how it projects itself toward the prey and utilizes its inner strength and gifts.

Let us start off with an interesting question: Who is the person you have the most influence on in your life?

You might come up with a number of answers, which could be your spouse, child or children, girl/boyfriend, parents, siblings or perhaps your best friend. BUT the person, whether you like it or not, that you have the most influence on and always will is...YOU! In addition, you are also the most important, because without love and compassion for yourself, how will you be able to give it to anyone else?

For many people this concept does not make sense, because more often than not, we look outside of ourselves and feel influenced, or like a victim of our environment.

Be assured that my goal is to make you even more aware that you have the ability to influence yourself in the way you desire, and from there, you can influence the people closest to you. You have influence on how you respond to your environment. You already have a couple of tools to help extend your awareness, which will come in handy in addition to what we've begun to discuss here.

You know from the study of The Stickman that we can consciously choose what we want to reject or allow into our lives. Since that's how it is for every single person on the planet, we must be able to conclude that we, theoretically, as individuals, have full and complete influence over ourselves, at least potentially. We must have the most influence on who we are, because we, as individuals, are solely responsible for all we think, say, do and believe. Influence is either self-imposed, or taken in by what we experience from our environment consciously or unconsciously.

So the first inner circle is you and me, the person we without a doubt have the most influence on and who is responsible for all we think, feel and do. Only we can make changes to ourselves when we discover we have to or want to in the pursuit of improving our lives in the way we choose. In a nutshell, we have to start with ourselves and begin from that starting point. Then we will work our way from the inside of ourselves and be the influence we desire to experience.

Second Phase

In the initial question of whom you influence most in your life, if you came up with the answer of a person close to you, then the answers in this second part of "the circle of influence" will have great relevance. Even though we have less influence on anyone else in our life, we do have a significant part in these relationships in terms of how we behave and so on.

The people you are influencing with your presence is every single person you encounter every day, whether it be family members, spouse or partner, children, friends, people you meet on the street or anyone you encounter. You now know that they, like you, have full responsibility of their actions from thoughts to feelings to actions, what they say and do and so on. However, they might not be aware of this and you might have a higher awareness that you can utilize, and therefore, be of positive influence the more you practice and develop these ideas.

Questions that might come to mind could be some of the following: Do we have an influence on if our friend comes on time to meet us, or does your manager have an influence on if you get to work on time, for that matter? If you are a salesman, do you have an influence on if the customer buys from you? And as a parent, do you have an influence on if your child does his or her chores?

The answer is YES! We have influence, but we do not have "control." You and I have the ability to choose what we want to do regardless of what the people around us say. We can decide to respect an agreed upon time, or get to work when our manager expects us to be there at a certain time.

Of course a salesman has influence over the customer buying, but there is no way the salesmen can force a purchase to secure his commission. In the same vein, a child wants to do the chores if s/he feels it may be a good idea and there is value in them.

One of the many truths that I believe is no matter how we travel on our unique journey, who we meet, who and what we learn from, the following quote seems to be the one that makes the most sense in terms of waking up to certain things in life, the influence we have on other people and the influence other people have on us, but it falls short because: "People will not believe something before they discover it for themselves." ~ Billy Sharp

We have a personal presence with the people we are around, and our presence often determines the outcome. If a person with immense, beautiful and great energy enters a room, that single person can raise the entire vibration for every person in that room, not by force or control, but of influence of how this individual feels about himself. Have you ever experienced this kind of energy?

Have you heard the saying about how you cannot force a horse to drink? You can lead the horse to water, but in no way can you force the horse to drink anything. It will start to drink when it's thirsty.

If you go to the store to buy some gum, and a cashier helps you with the purchase, you both have influence in these moments. The person with the higher vibration will pull up the other one. If that person is down, you can smile, pat her/him on the shoulder and say "I hope you have a great day!"

There are ways to influence any person we encounter and it will always start from inside of ourselves with how we feel about who we are as individuals, how we love and enjoy ourselves. Our energy will be carried out into the atmosphere and have an influence everywhere we are with any person. You have influence on yourself and that will be the way to gain influence on how people behave toward you. It is quite beautiful and simple. In given situations, we tend not to have the patience or awareness, and rather we want to have everything controlled. This creates a lot of resistance, since it is not possible to control any person. No one should be controlled! Every person has her/his own uniqueness and way of living. The mutual influence is the gift of raising both the uniqueness and way of living to a higher and more constructive place, especially if at least one person or perhaps both people are aware of their mutual influence.

So the main point of this second phase of influence is to know that you have influence on any encounter with any individual, regardless of the relationship. It is vital to know that you are always in a sphere of influence and have a responsibility to how you are involved in it. You are not in control nor should you force anything, yourself included. From that last sentence, what I have learned is control is resistance and what resists persists, so it is a tug of war, and therefore, unpleasant.

In other words, be the influence you wish to experience.

So to conclude these two phases, we know that the person we have the most influence on is ourselves. From there we have less influence on a relative basis, with any person we meet. It is vital to take the following into account, that when you are physically present, you are an influence and you have an influence on the mutual experience with the person in front of you.

The Third Phase

Now, we'll move into an area where we do not have much influence or any at all. Even though the science of quantum mechanics tells us we are one with all there is, and therefore, we are connected with everything in the universe, I do believe from an individual standpoint, we do not have enough of an influence to change the course of certain things. For example, we do not have the influence to change the weather, the car accident on the other side of the planet, your friend who gets laid off from her/his job, or the computer system at your work that doesn't function.

What you do have influence on is HOW you respond to situations, such as rain on your wedding day or the robbery that just happened. We can tap ourselves dry of energy by being frustrated on a continuous basis with what is out of our control. The only thing we can "control" or have influence on is our behavioral response. As difficult as it may seem, situations that are out of our control provide us with an opportunity of choice in how we will respond and what energy we will put into these situations. We have to realize what we have an impact on and what we don't. Our gift is letting go of situations we can't control and focusing our energy on what we can control. This gift frees us.

Does this mean we should not be upset, sad or frustrated during certain times in our lives? For example, if one of our loved ones passes away, if we get laid off from our current position or our sibling was in a serious car accident? No, because sadness is a natural part of life. Understanding our influence brings us the awareness of what we are not in control of and the ability to deal with such situations in a different way, with more awareness and ease.

From the inside out we have influence and the more we understand our influence, the stronger we will feel and more confident we will be in our encounters.

Reaction vs. Response

Look at the image on the second page of this chapter because much of what we are talking about here comes down to how we react, and/or how we respond. Reaction is not grounded, but typically unconscious behavior, which is triggered and a by-product of an action you are doing. Reactions are not conscious behavior.

On the other hand, a response is to put who you are in the situation and take what you have inside and be a conscious influence. Being grounded and in balance with yourself will be a natural outcome, if you are responding to your environment. It is very positive to be in this state because it is an expression of being present with the situations you are in. When you listen intently in a conversation you are already responding, because you are paying close attention and reasoning with the information being given. If you were just hearing it and searching for something negative that didn't fit with your beliefs, you would most likely react verbally or with a closed mind. And the conversation could be cut short.

We have to trust ourselves in how we live and respond to our circumstances. We must stand up for who we are, as the unique individuals we are. The more we recognize and realize about ourselves, the more compassion and love we will find. In turn we can express our own passion and love in our environment more naturally.

Be aware of your influence on yourself and the people around you. Always keep with you the idea of responding to what you don't have much or any control over.

Make sure that from now on you will become the influence you wish to experience. You have the ability and responsibility from the inside out to make it so, for yourself and the world around you.

This does not mean you will be perfect, but your goal should be to raise awareness within yourself, for you to bring along on your unique journey, since you are constantly a work in progress. Although imperfection can improve infinitely and bring you closer to perfection, ironically, perfection always seems to be out of your grasp. This is a blessing for us to understand that we can never reach this "point" of perfection. Life and who we are is a continually growing process. We are always learning, growing and striving for a fulfilled life. And if we're doing all of these things, we're headed in the right direction.

Exercise #4: Turning Reaction Into Response

The exercise that follows is a completely free and optional opportunity. I want you to feel free to do it whenever you want and only if you want. I find that if I tell you to do this exercise before you move onto the next chapter, you might feel it is blocking you from continuing to read if you're in a flow. That is why you should do it when you have the inspiration and desire to do so. That way you will receive the most out of the exercise.

The exercise is to help you find answers inside of yourself and be able to express them. It will make you more aware of your findings. Then you can progress by understanding yourself and creating more clarity.

The way we know what kind of influence we are in any place or any situation is by sitting down and consciously reflecting. We should reflect on how we behave toward ourselves or in a situation toward any person or in any way. We should also be brutally honest about our actions.

At the end of the day, you can reflect on everything that has happened. From when you awoke to when you went to work and talked to people or anywhere else. You can also take a full week or a month and reflect on it in as much detail as possible by examining as many instances and situations as possible. Then you can evaluate how you behaved toward yourself or situations, how your influence impacted these situations and each person you encountered and how long you were in the given environment.

This exercise will open you up to how you begin to see yourself and how you react and respond to everything that happens. The more you become aware of your reactions and responses, the more you will begin to see and observe yourself in how you behave and what influence and feeling you get from every situation. You will learn to be more aware of the way you feel and why you feel this way. Plus, the result will be more conscious awareness about your own behavior in and around situations and people as you gradually improve.

So...decide to reflect on yesterday, last week or maybe the past month. You can, of course, reflect on very specific situations in your life, which have had a big impact. Choose what you feel like and dig deep within yourself. Think about the reactions you've had or often have on a daily basis that you want to turn into more responsive ways of being.

If you need to write down your reflections, then do so. Reflection and turning reactions into more responsive behavior is a key in communication and relationships toward yourself and what and who you encounter in your life.

_____

_____

_____

_____

_____

_____

_____

_____

Head to Heart Tool

"The longest journey is the twenty inches from the head to the heart."

~ ANCIENT PROVERB

Why is it that when we are in a state of doubt or confusion, people advise us to "follow your heart?" Is it a coincidence that in this area of our body, this organ, we tend to put our focus? I mean, how often do you hear, "follow your head"?

We know the saying: "You can do anything you put your mind to." It's true, although it is leading us to a strong emotion, which we then follow. This is where our heart enters the picture more profoundly.

At times we ponder what kind of decisions to make, at a given time in our lives. We weigh our options, relating what we've experienced in the past. Then we waver on what actions to take based on our past experiences. When this occurs, we are in our head, and it can easily cause confusion. This sentence goes along well with this idea: "When you think long you think wrong." Basically, there's no need to overanalyze everything, so remember: Don't give it too much thought.

When we have a strong feeling and passion for something we really want to pursue with our heart, we intuitively know what we want. We know what that is and it allows us to follow our passion, our fire. Therefore, in those scenarios, simply follow this feeling, and it won't be a decision.

We are constantly bombarded by thoughts, which are mere illusions, but we often allow them in and make them "real." We allow them to have a major impact on our lives. Our head stores everything we have experienced. We compare our negative and destructive experiences from the past to our present circumstances. They may not correlate with each other at all, but we still bring our past of doubt and fear of the future into the present. This negative thought pattern ruins the present, which is the only place where we can make changes and take action. In essence, it is what blocks us from heartfelt progress, because we get in our own way.

Why do thoughts have such a tremendous impact? The reality is that thoughts do not have an impact until we give them the power to make it so. Shakespeare has a fantastic quote: "Nothing is good or bad, but thinking makes it so." I want to take that a step further and say that everything is what it is, until our thinking makes it what we make it out to be. And as you know by now, we have the choice at all times.

Our thoughts will often feel heavy and difficult when we enter a totally new phase in our lives and/or we go to places we've never been. And as you already know, we have to enter something new to grow. The following quote, one of my favorites, which you've heard a few times now, concludes this concept beautifully: "If you want to go somewhere you have not gone before, you have to do something you have not done before."

With all the knowledge you've acquired reading this book, it's time to discuss the key to having a more fulfilled life. Please do not expect that just because you know the key after reading this that you will live it right away. That certainly would be a long shot, because in my opinion, it's the longest journey you can ever begin. I am where you are; no one is perfect. I am a work in progress on my unique journey, doing what I can to be more and more in tune with my heart.

Our head and heart have obvious significance, since our brain is the most incredible machine in the universe and our heart is the most powerful energy center we have. In the scientific community, evidence shows that our heart has a magnetic field, which is 5000 times stronger than our brains. The connection between these two centers is vital. The more our brain and heart connect, the better the functioning of our entire being; this state is called: coherence.

The definitions of coherence are:

- The quality or state of cohering, especially a logical, orderly and aesthetically consistent relationship of parts;
- Physics: The property of being coherent, as of waves;
- Logical or natural connection or consistency.

(Source: http://www.thefreedictionary.com/coherence)

When reading the above, what does coherence mean to you, in regard to your heart and brain?

To me, it means that if coherence is created out of a consistent and natural relationship with two significant parts, it's about time to connect the two and live through them as one. Our life will be more fulfilled when this occurs, wouldn't you agree? For example, when we feel oneness in a conversation, in a friendship or a loving relationship, it feels so much better than if we are experiencing separation.

If we flip the focus to our heart, energy will establish this powerful connection from heart to head and connect the actual coherence we desire, and the result is, that we will know it as soon as it happens. And believe me, you will know when it happens.

For instance, I was at a conference in Chicago in June of 2011. On the last day of the conference, I attended a full-day lecture with Gregg Braden. He is a phenomenal author, speaker and person to say the least. Everyone in the audience, including me observed how a heart rate device worked and how it established coherence between the head and heart by focusing on the heart for a few minutes.

It seems that, if we focus on our heart, the coherence, which helps us with creativity, inspiration, affection, love and compassion toward ourselves, life and the people around us, originates from our heart. It seems obvious, but when experienced, it gives a greater awareness to this fact.

So I believe that the way to be in a more coherent state is not necessarily to take away from what this quote conveys: "The longest journey is the twenty inches from the head to the heart." It is simply to understand the heart is where the journey and change have to be lived from and take place. Then we will create and re-establish this beautiful relationship between heart and brain, which is already natural. It has to be reconnected on a more constant basis again, which will happen with the more focus and attention we give it.

I want you to see your head and brain as your ultimate tools for navigation on your journey. From studying the tools you have so far, such as The Stickman, Comfort Zone, Circle of Influence, six mental tools, etc., you now have a higher awareness of yourself than before reading this book. This combination of tools will help you navigate your way through your personal journey.

All of the above helps move our physical body that we are solely responsible for, purposely in the direction we desire. It all helps us in getting better in following our heart, in what is a daily practice on a long journey. Many people say that we are here for a short time, and perhaps we are, but I believe the more conscious we are of our life as we live it right now, the longer and more joyful it will feel. Life can then feel like a long and amazing ride!

The overall pursuit is to be in tune with our hearts, but how is this possible? And what kind of promise does this have?

On the road, as we walk it, we will gradually find what works for us and what doesn't. We will find out what we like and dislike. We will find out what makes us tick and what doesn't and what we have a passion and love for, which only happens when we encounter what does not make us feel good. This is where we learn and develop confidence and courage in what direction we want to go.

No one can teach you something you have not lived or experienced yet. We can prepare in all sorts of ways with all sorts of people and on top of that, obtain a backpack of tools to take with us. We can accumulate items along the way that work for us, but we have to walk our own path and take the punches and swings as we go. We cannot do anything or get anywhere completely alone. We will need support from family, friends and partners, but since we are unique and have such an existence, it is important to understand that we all have our own unique journey.

I want to recommend a really great book that to my knowledge is not famous or legendary, although it should be. It is a genuine explanation of the shadows lurking in the environment of personal development and spirituality. The name of the book is *Shadows On The Path* by Abdi Assadi. There is something about the title that is quite fitting to what we are talking about here, in terms of the idea of our journey. I urge you to read this book, because it delves into the reality of life, which often is neglected when something or someone is put on a pedestal. The sad thing is so much knowledge and so many personalities are put up there. This belief is superficial and short–lived, like a leaf without a branch and tree to keep it alive.

What Assadi's book helped me understand combined with what my life has taught me is there is NO ABSOLUTE answer that fits every person. The answer that fits every person is the answer we find for ourselves, when we through our trials and struggles wake up to the unique individual we are and find peace with who we are…when we stop looking out and trying to find answers from other people and comparing ourselves to everyone. Instead we begin to find the love that resides inside and, we express and utilize that unique gift, which is being a unique human being, but also in what we can share and give to the world. By knowing and living this truth, I believe we have found some of the essentials in life. We can only know these essentials when we live consciously, and that experience is, if you haven't already guessed it, unique!

Heartmath

Heartmath is a science, which creates evidence around what we are talking about here, when it comes to the connection between the heart and head and how healthy it is to become aware of the aspects of this connection.

Heartmath scientists created a device called the emWave, which you can either put in the computer and use or carry around with you. Through collected data, which is accumulated through your breathing and pulse shown on the screen via graphs, games and so forth, it shows what state you are in, whether it is close or far from the coherent state. It provides evidence of how much focus you have on being and living from your heart. Through practice it gives you a great awareness of knowing when you either are or aren't in a productive state that is serving you and feels good.

I urge you to visit www.heartmath.com to find out more.

I believe it is everyone´s pursuit to be and live from our heart, because we all know how that feels, whether we've felt it with our parents, family, friends, pets, etc.

And the journey from our head to our heart is definitely a long one, and forever ongoing. So if you are ever in some kind of doubt, follow your heart and go forward.

Exercise #5: Ways to An Open Heart

The exercise that follows is a completely free and optional opportunity. I want you to feel free to do it whenever you want and only if you want. I find that if I tell you to do this exercise right now, you might feel it is blocking you from continuing to read if you're in a flow. That is why you should do it when you have the inspiration and desire to do so. That way you will receive the most out of the exercise.

The exercise is to help you find answers inside of yourself and be able to express them. It will make you more aware of your findings. Then you can progress by understanding yourself and creating more clarity.

I have two ways and ideas to potentially bring you closer to living from your heart. These are, of course, optional and to help give you some additional tools. You will find out if these tools work for you or not, but I feel it is important to share what I believe can help you.

These two exercises will help you move into a more coherent state.

Hand or hands on heart

Place one or both hands on your heart and feel your heart pound. Give your heart attention. I usually put both of my hands on my heart because it has more warmth and energy, and in my experience helps me connect the mind and heart into a coherent state.

The objective is to feel more relaxed and calm, and to be free from racing thoughts or any type of stressful or confused state. You will enter into a state that is far more enjoyable, peaceful and has a more beautiful type of energy, which is healthy, feels good and makes you happy. You will then be able to express yourself as who you are, feel creative and inspired and all the great feelings that come along with it.

In my experience, it takes us varying amounts of time for the calm to descend upon us, and that's okay. We all move at different speeds. Try the exercise and see how it goes. You will know when you are in more of a coherent state.

What Would Love Do?

This is an exercise similar to the first one, and one you can do anywhere as long as you are conscious of it. I read a book a few years ago, and in the particular section I was reading, the author talked about love. We all know when we feel and experience what we have related to the word "love." Love has a different meaning for everyone. In general, it's a strong and comfortable feeling, one in which we always feel good, do good things for ourselves and others in a very natural way when we are in the state of love.

That brings us to this question: When we feel an emotion that does not feel pleasant, comfortable or positive: <u>What would love do?</u> Give It A Shot!

A quick additional exercise is to come up with a specific situation in your life. For example, maybe today an argument arose with your spouse, or maybe an instance that caused some kind

78

of negative emotion or behavior a while ago that you remember because of its impact. Look back and ask yourself the question: What would love do in that situation?

Don't put yourself in this equation, just think about what love would do and how that situation could have turned out if we had utilized the idea of love instead. This exercise is to make you see and realize the potential for a better outcome when we proceed through life with love in our hearts. In addition, it can teach us valuable lessons, since this kind of love is something inherent to us, and we have what it takes to alter outcomes when we respond from the place of love.

Final Notes & Thank You

My purpose through this book has been to reveal your own uniqueness. I hope I have given you something to work with and work on.

Has something changed for you while reading this book?

I believe, as I've mentioned so many times, that one of the most important keys in life is to open ourselves up and embrace our uniqueness. By sharing and utilizing this gift, we will be able to give it to all other unique individuals. Look at how much information you can receive and how many great things you can experience by being open to uniqueness. You will only experience the unique journey you are on, and since everyone is on her/his own journey, there is so much to learn from everyone you meet on your way. Be open to mutual uniqueness, because everyone has gone through something and that's a valuable lesson. What a gift that is, huh?

What we share together is that we are all on a unique journey through life and that is what will bring us together. When we are aware of this fact, we bring each other into one another's lives by understanding this concept of uniqueness.

We are all students and teachers on every level. It is our purpose to come together and utilize the uniqueness in the skills and personalities we all have.

Thank you

I want to sincerely thank you for reading this book. I certainly hope that it has provided you with information that is of value to your life. Remember that you are unique and that is what makes us all equal to each other.

Thanks again, and I look forward to being in touch with you, and if I can help you in any way, please let me know.

May you be well and safe on Your Unique Journey!

About The Author

Gideon Nielsen is twenty seven years of age and was born in Copenhagen, Denmark. Gideon is a certified LifeSuccess Consultant, and a person who sees his life experience as his education. Through his impeccable passion for improving himself by reading and writing as well as developing himself tirelessly, he has gained the fascination of studying people and life.

He is often told that he is wise beyond his years and many call him an "old soul." He is not afraid of jumping out into the unknown with only a parachute. He has faith in landing and takes life as it comes, no matter where it leads to or what it will be. In this way, he lives with confidence and vision. He lives on the edge of his comfort zone in a consistent pursuit to explore life and himself.

Since February 15th, 2010, he has lived out of his green backpack, using only what he can fit in it. His travels have taken him to countries like Australia, Canada, Costa Rica, Norway, the United States and Mexico. While he was in Costa Rica, the United States and Canada, he attended a variety of conferences, workshops and seminars, where he has developed a large and reliable network. His kindness and openness toward people and life make it interesting to meet Gideon if you ever get the chance.

His journey inside of himself and around the world has developed many ideas, including founding the ideas of the project named Your Unique Journey. His work as the Journey Navigator culminated in this book.

His vision is to bring all of us together through understanding our individual uniqueness and the journey we are on, and to share and inspire each other through this journey called life.

Who knows where he will be next? Maybe he will be crossing paths with you somewhere, sometime…

Offer From The Journey Navigator!

By having a copy of this book in either paperback or e-book, you have one free 30-minute coaching call available to you!

I am giving you this opportunity, because if this book helped you, you might desire to get in touch with me personally to receive more guidance.

If you want to take advantage of this opportunity, all you have to do is to write me an email at the address below. When you do, put in the subject line the following text: "I Want A Free 30-minute Unique Coaching Call." And we will get the call set up.

I look forward to hearing from you!

Contact Me

If you feel Y<u>our</u> Unique Journey has enriched your life, and you would like to get in touch with me, please do. Shoot me an email or friend me:

By email: GideonNielsen@gmail.com

Visit my website: www.Journey-Navigator.com

Visit my blog: www.GideonsUniqueJourney.com

Support my project: www.YourUniqueJourney.com

Facebook: www.facebook.com/GideonsJourney

Want To Share Your Story?

Everybody has an inspiring story. I want to read about your story. My project: *Your Unique Journey* is collecting stories from everyone who wants to share a story from their life´s journey with the world. To share your story, please visit: www.YourUniqueJourney.com.